WORLD STUDIES
OCEANIA

by Marie Pearson

T0025170

FOCUS READERS.

VOYAGER

www.focusreaders.com

Focus Readers is distributed by North Star Editions:
sales@northstareditions.com | 888-417-0195

Produced for Focus Readers by Red Line Editorial.

Content Consultant: Sylvia Frain, PhD, Auckland University of Technology, Vakatele Pacific Research Network, The University of Guam Micronesian Area Research Center

Photographs ©: Shutterstock Images, cover, 1, 4–5, 7, 15, 16–17, 27, 31, 33, 43; Michael Long/Science Source, 8–9; David Rumsey Historical Map Collection, 11; Department of the Interior/US Fish and Wildlife Service/Bureau of Commercial Fisheries/Woods Hole Laboratory (1956–1970)/US National Archives and Records Administration, 13; Jorge Silva/Reuters/Newscom, 18; iStockphoto, 20–21, 23, 24; Michael S. Nolan/robertharding/Newscom, 28–29; Rod McGuirk/AP Images, 34–35; Dita Alangkara/AP Images, 37; Michael Runkel/robertharding/Alamy, 38; Danita Delimont Photography/Newscom, 40–41; Caleb Jones/AP Images, 45

Library of Congress Cataloging-in-Publication Data
Names: London, Martha, author.
Title: Oceania / by Martha London.
Description: Lake Elmo, MN : Focus Readers, [2021] | Series: World studies | Includes index. | Audience: Grades 7-9
Identifiers: LCCN 2019057383 (print) | LCCN 2019057384 (ebook) | ISBN 9781644934029 (hardcover) | ISBN 9781644934784 (paperback) | ISBN 9781644936306 (pdf) | ISBN 9781644935545 (ebook)
Subjects: LCSH: Oceania--Juvenile literature.
Classification: LCC DU17 .L66 2021 (print) | LCC DU17 (ebook) | DDC 995--dc23
LC record available at https://lccn.loc.gov/2019057383
LC ebook record available at https://lccn.loc.gov/2019057384

Printed in the United States of America
Mankato, MN
012021

ABOUT THE AUTHOR

Martha London writes books for young readers. When she isn't writing, you can find her hiking in the woods.

TABLE OF CONTENTS

CHAPTER 1

WELCOME TO OCEANIA

The southern part of the Pacific Ocean is vast and deep. This area, which stretches from Southeast Asia to the Americas, is dotted with islands large and small. This area is called Oceania. Its many islands and people share a relationship to the ocean.

More than 10,000 islands fill Oceania. They are roughly divided into four regions. These areas are Australia, Melanesia, Micronesia, and Polynesia.

Less than 10 percent of Oceania is land. The rest is ocean.

The regions of Oceania are separated by features of the earth. For example, a chain of volcanoes runs through Oceania. It separates Melanesia from Micronesia and Polynesia.

Oceania is home to 14 countries. It is also home to other territories, such as Guam. In these territories, people do not have full control over their government. The United Nations calls these places non-self-governing territories. Guam is a single island in Micronesia. Other countries and territories have hundreds of islands.

Australia has the highest population of any country in Oceania. It is also one of the largest countries in the world by area. Australia has several urban centers along its coast. Very few people live in the middle of the country.

New Zealand also has a large population. This country is part of Polynesia. New Zealand is made up of two main islands. Its largest cities are on the North Island. The South Island is mostly rural. Hawaii is part of Polynesia as well. Hawaii's native peoples have a close cultural connection to other native peoples of Oceania, such as the Māori in New Zealand. Māori call their land Aotearoa.

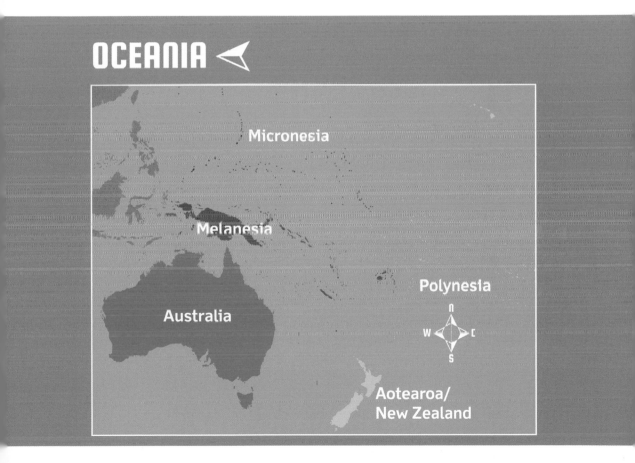

OCEANIA ◅

Micronesia

Melanesia

Australia

Polynesia

N
W ◅◆► E
S

Aotearoa/
New Zealand

HISTORY OF OCEANIA

Tens of thousands of years ago, Australia, Tasmania, and New Guinea were fused together. This landmass was called Sahul. Humans came to Sahul at least 40,000 years ago. These peoples quickly spread throughout Sahul.

Approximately 8,000 years ago, sea levels rose. This rise created the landmasses people recognize today. Ocean waters split Tasmania, Australia, and New Guinea into separate lands.

When people first came to Sahul, massive marsupials lived on the continent.

Thousands of years later, a second wave of people arrived in Oceania. These people came from Southeast Asia. By 1500 BCE, they had reached islands in Micronesia and Melanesia. They met Papuan peoples in New Guinea. They also settled the Solomon Islands. By 1000 BCE, people had reached the Polynesian islands of Tonga and Samoa. Later explorers went north to Hawaii. Others went farther east to Easter Island.

Great distances separated people in Polynesia. Even so, people developed trading systems with one another. By the 1200s CE, Polynesian people had traveled farther south. They reached Aotearoa, or New Zealand. These people were the ancestors of modern Māori.

European settlers did not arrive in Oceania until the early 1500s. In the late 1700s, British settlers set up their first **colony** in Australia.

⏺ Early people in Oceania built strong canoes. These ships could cross thousands of miles of water.

Europeans wanted the region's resources, such as gold and whales. They also wanted to enslave Oceania's people. Many more colonies followed.

During the 1800s, British colonists took over all of Australia and New Zealand. The Dutch took over much of New Guinea. The French took several islands in Polynesia. And US colonists took much of Hawaii, Guam, and American Samoa.

In addition, Europeans brought diseases with them. **Indigenous** people's bodies had not been exposed to these diseases before. Hundreds of thousands died as a result. Violence was also common. In Australia, British colonists killed at least 20,000 First Nations people.

Even so, Indigenous peoples resisted these settlers. In the mid-1800s, Māori peoples fought against New Zealand forces over their land. And Tonga remained independent until 1900.

In the 1900s, European control weakened. Australia and New Zealand gradually gained independence from the United Kingdom. Still,

> **THINK ABOUT IT**
>
> Indigenous peoples in Oceania have faced hundreds of years of violence and control from non-native people. Do you know of any similar histories where you live?

Between 1946 and 1958, the US military tested 23 nuclear bombs at Bikini Atoll in Micronesia.

Indigenous peoples faced other forms of control. For example, during World War I (1914–1918), Japan took over many islands in Micronesia.

World War II (1939–1945) brought massive change to Oceania. Many battles took place in the region. After the war, the United States and France used the region for nuclear testing. This testing had harmful effects that remain through the present day. Many island-nations did gain independence. But as of 2020, several territories were still not independent.

MĀORI LANGUAGE

Māori are Indigenous to Aotearoa/New Zealand. Māori describes many different peoples. There are more than 60 iwi, or tribes. All iwi are unique. But there are some similarities between them. For example, Māori tend to speak one common language. This language is Te Reo Māori.

In the 1800s, the British government thought Māori should **assimilate**. It made English the official language of New Zealand. After 1871, no public schools used Te Reo Māori in their classes. Throughout the 1900s, fewer Māori people learned their native language. By the 1980s, fewer than 20 percent could speak Te Reo Māori.

Many Māori people believed their cultures were at risk. New Zealand's government agreed. In the 1980s, programs began helping Māori learn their language again. In 1987, the government made Te Reo Māori one of the country's official

▲ In 2017, there were approximately 734,000 Māori living in Aotearoa/New Zealand.

languages. Some schools began teaching some or all of their lessons in this language.

By the 2010s, more than 20 percent of Māori people in New Zealand could have a conversation in Te Reo Māori. The language was also growing elsewhere in New Zealand. Pop songs in Te Reo Māori became popular. And more TV stations began using the language. These shifts helped Māori stay connected to their cultures.

CHAPTER 3

GEOGRAPHY AND CLIMATE

Oceania covers nearly 40 million square miles (100 million sq km). Most of this area is ocean. Australia is the region's largest stretch of land. Much of this landmass is desert and grassland.

A variety of islands dot the waters of Oceania. New Zealand and New Guinea are continental islands. These types of islands were at one point attached to continents. Over time, they became separated from those larger masses of land.

The large area of desert and grassland in Australia is known as the Outback.

Rising sea levels can cause this separation. Higher levels of water can cover large areas of land. This water often separates some areas from others. When that happens, continental islands form.

Another type of island forms from the eruption of underground volcanoes. As the lava hardens, it builds up. Over millions of years, the lava rises above the surface of the ocean. It creates an island. Many of Oceania's islands no longer have active volcanoes. However, some do. For example, Vanuatu has several active volcanoes.

Coral islands are the smallest kind of island. The island itself is not made of coral. During storms, rock and sand get stuck in the coral. Over time, that material builds up to form an island. Thousands of coral islands exist in Oceania.

Despite the vast size of Oceania, only two main climates occur in the region. Some countries, such as New Zealand and Australia, have temperate climates. This type of climate does not have extreme temperatures. It has warm summers and cool winters. Other areas, such as Tahiti and the Solomon Islands, are tropical. They are warm all year and have a wet season and a dry season. Rainforests cover many of Oceania's tropical islands. They tend to receive large amounts of rain.

CHAPTER 4

PLANTS AND ANIMALS

Oceania is home to a huge variety of plants and animals. For example, marsupials such as kangaroos are mostly native to Oceania. These animals carry their babies in pouches.

Some of the region's animals do not exist anywhere else in the world. Echidnas and platypuses can only be found in Oceania. They are also the only two species of mammals that lay eggs. Echidnas live in forests and deserts.

Young kangaroos are known as joeys.

In contrast, platypuses are built for water. They use their bills to sift food from the bottoms of rivers and ponds. Their webbed feet make platypuses excellent swimmers.

Birds are among the most common types of animals in Oceania. One reason is the number of islands in the region. Few other animals can travel across Oceania. However, some of the world's largest flightless birds also live in Oceania. Some examples include the emu and cassowary. They live in Australia. The kiwi is another flightless bird. This small bird is native to New Zealand.

Many species of plants also grow in Oceania. The area's wet climates support massive plant **biodiversity**. For instance, approximately 1,200 plant species are native to Hawaii. More than 80 percent of those species are found nowhere else on Earth.

▲ The texture and scent of breadfruit are often compared to fresh bread.

One important plant in Oceania is the breadfruit. People brought these plants with them as they explored islands across Oceania. On each island, they planted breadfruit trees. A single breadfruit tree can produce 200 pounds (90 kg) of fruit each year. The wood is also good for building shelters and boats.

▲ Algae that live inside corals often give corals their colors.

The land biomes of Oceania are not the only places with biodiversity. The ocean contains a number of huge ecosystems. Tens of thousands of kinds of animals swim the waters. For example, many whale sharks travel to the west coast of

Australia every spring. Whale sharks are the largest fish on Earth.

Much of Earth's marine life lives in coral reefs. Coral might look like plants. But they are actually animals. Two of the largest reefs in the world exist in Oceania. The Great Barrier Reef is located off the coast of Australia. Kingman Reef is 900 miles (1,400 km) from Hawaii. Both are protected wildlife refuges. The Kingman Reef has a narrow **atoll** that is above the water. The atoll provides nesting grounds for sea turtles and seabirds. Seabirds such as the gannet and rockhopper penguin rely on the fish that live near coral reefs.

Reefs provide shelter and food to many species of marine animals. Reefs also create a natural barrier between the ocean and land. During storms, waves crash against the reef instead of flooding the island. This protects people and land.

THE GREAT BARRIER REEF

The Great Barrier Reef looks like one long reef. But it is actually 3,000 reefs. The reef system covers 1,600 miles (2,500 km). The Great Barrier Reef is so large that it can be seen from space.

Like all coral reefs, the Great Barrier Reef is home to many species of marine life. Mollusks, fish, whales, and turtles live in the water. Birds and plants live on the coral that reaches above the surface. And the reef itself is made of more than 600 types of coral.

A coral reef is made of living animals. It is always changing. The Great Barrier Reef has existed off Australia's coast for 500,000 years. But its shape depends on water levels and climate. The current shape is less than 10,000 years old.

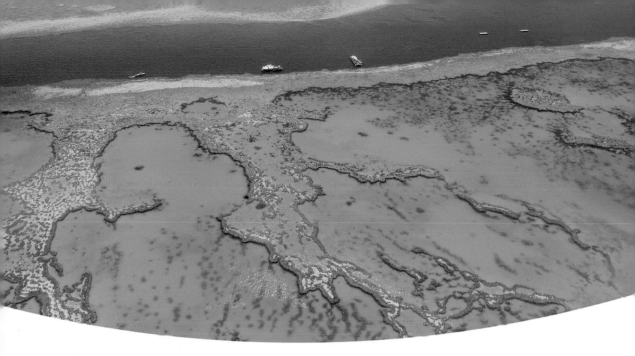

Many scientists worry that climate change will destroy the Great Barrier Reef completely by 2050.

More than three million people visit the Great Barrier Reef each year. However, the reef faces major threats. One of the largest threats is climate change. This crisis is harming the reef in many ways, including raising ocean water temperatures. Coral can only survive in certain temperatures.

Scientists are working to help the reef. And people can slow climate change. But to save the Great Barrier Reef, much more action is needed.

CHAPTER 5

NATURAL RESOURCES AND ECONOMY

Oceania has many resources. They support the region in a variety of ways. For example, nearly all of Oceania's islands have farms. Most islands are too small to grow export crops, or crops sold to other countries. Many people produce food only for their own communities. They grow a lot of fruit, such as bananas and coconuts. Australia can sell its crops overseas. Beef and wheat are two of its largest exports.

A Paumotu person chops a coconut on Niau Atoll in French Polynesia.

Australia is also one of the world's largest producers of gold. Most of the country's gold mines are in Western Australia. Mining is important in other parts of Oceania, too. New Zealand, Fiji, and the Solomon Islands mine a variety of metals. These metals include iron, lead, and nickel. The world's largest copper and gold mine is in Papua New Guinea.

Not all mining is for metal, however. In Papua New Guinea, a US company mines natural gas. This gas is a common energy source. In New Zealand, some companies mine pumice. This rock comes from volcanoes. People use pumice to smooth their feet.

Oceania's large islands also rely on their lumber industries. New Zealand is one of the world's top exporters of timber. Papua New Guinea exports eucalyptus, pine, and rosewood.

▲ In 2018, New Zealand exported much of its timber to China.

Indigenous Papuan peoples own nearly all the island's forests. Certain groups own different parts of the forests. All permits for cutting must be approved by those groups.

Many smaller islands depend on fishing. And countries around the world buy fish from Oceania. For example, the region supplies most of the world's tuna. Many islands also have rights to the ocean around them. They control who can use the water for large-scale fishing.

In addition, Oceania's economies often depend on outside nations. China has become especially important for many of these economies. For example, the Solomon Islands sells most of its exports to China. China has also loaned large amounts of money to several islands, including Tonga and Fiji.

The US military also remains important to certain islands. The US military provides jobs for many people in the region, including in Guam. Military spending is also Guam's largest industry. In Hawaii, the military is the second-largest industry. Only tourism plays a larger role.

> ## THINK ABOUT IT

What are the advantages of tourism in small island-nations? What are the disadvantages?

An Indigenous Cook Islander leads an ecotour to visitors on the island of Rarotonga in Polynesia.

In fact, tourism is a massive part of many Oceanian economies. The area's climate and beaches draw millions of visitors every year. For example, Palau is an island in Micronesia. Tourists there tend to outnumber the local population. But the government works to keep the country healthy. It requires visitors to sign a pledge to respect the land and water. This type of ecotourism is growing across Oceania.

CHAPTER 6

GOVERNMENT AND POLITICS

Governments in Oceania vary widely. Some are based on the countries that took the areas over. For example, Australia's and New Zealand's governments resemble the United Kingdom's government. Representatives run these countries' **parliamentary democracies**. Citizens vote for those representatives to serve in Parliament.

Other countries also use a British model of government. Many of them are in Melanesia.

Papua New Guinea's prime minister (left) meets with Australia's prime minister in July 2019.

Indigenous peoples tend to control these governments fully. However, in New Zealand, only some seats are reserved for Māori people. And few First Nations people have ever served in Australia's government.

Certain islands remain more connected to outside countries. Hawaii, for example, is a US state. Many Micronesian nations are also connected to the United States. The Federated States of Micronesia (FSM) is one example. FSM citizens can work and live freely in the United States. However, people from Hawaii are US citizens. People from the FSM are not.

In contrast, people from Guam are US citizens. But Guam is a US territory, not a state. Guam's citizens have fewer rights than other US citizens. New Zealand and France also control these kinds of non-self-governing territories.

West Papuan students protest for independence in August 2019.

Indonesia's control over West Papua is especially strong. West Papua is on the same island as Papua New Guinea. But Indonesia has controlled West Papua for decades. Papuans often face racism and violence from the Indonesian military. Papuans have protested for independence for decades.

In addition, Oceania's large countries are often at odds with the region's small island-nations.

In 2019, sea-level rise caused by climate change was already affecting two of Tuvalu's nine islands.

For instance, these small islands were among the first places harmed by climate change. As a result, many of them have led the movement against this crisis. Even so, Australia's and New Zealand's pollution levels rose in the 2010s. In response, Fiji's president and others tried to pressure those countries. They wanted these large countries to take more action against climate change.

News outlets have criticized Australia in other ways. One way is how it uses smaller islands. For certain periods in the 2000s, the Australian government put strict limits on the number of **refugees** allowed into the country. Instead, it sent these people to the islands of Nauru and Manus. The government forced them to stay in detention centers. Some people have been held there for several years.

Many countries in Oceania face issues of **migration**. People move between islands for work opportunities. Natural disasters force others to leave their homes. Climate change will make many kinds of movement more common. For these reasons, governments are trying to better manage migration into and out of their countries.

THINK ABOUT IT ◁

Conflicts between small and large countries are common in Oceania. Why might this be? Do you notice these kinds of conflicts in other parts of the world?

CHAPTER 7

PEOPLE AND CULTURE

Oceania's peoples are diverse. Many cultures exist within one region. Micronesia is one example. Chamorro people live in Guam and the Commonwealth of the Northern Mariana Islands (CNMI). Guam's culture mixes Indigenous, Spanish, Filipino, and US traditions. The CNMI are larger islands known as high islands. But people also live on the area's atolls. Low-island people have different cultures than the high islanders.

John "Big John" Tedtaotao, a Chamorro man, rides a water buffalo in the village of Umatac in Guam.

For this reason, some experts believe Micronesia is not a useful name. They argue the area's cultures are too different from one another. Some believe the name Melanesia is also too broad. After all, these labels came about only after Europeans arrived. And more than 1,300 languages are spoken in Melanesia.

At the same time, millions of people in Melanesia speak a common **pidgin** language. This shared language helped form a shared identity. In part, this identity celebrates the differences among people. Music often gives voice to this idea. The region's music tends to have roots in native traditions. But it also draws on other kinds of music, such as hip-hop or reggae.

In certain ways, people in Polynesia have more in common. These people used canoes to travel the ocean for thousands of years. Since the 1970s, a Hawaiian group has brought back this art. Mau Piailug, a Micronesian navigator, provided this group with his knowledge. The group helps people get closer to their culture. In this way, the ocean connects many different peoples to one another.

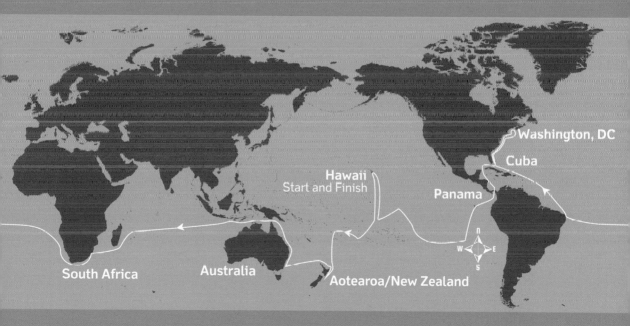

THE MĀLAMA HONUA VOYAGE ◄

Between 2013 and 2017, an Indigenous crew sailed west around the world in a traditional canoe to bring awareness to climate change. In Hawaiian, the voyage's name means "to care for our Earth."

Washington, DC

Cuba

Hawaii
Start and Finish

Panama

South Africa

Australia

Aotearoa/New Zealand

Land often brings groups together, too. For example, the Kanaka Maoli people are native to Hawaii. The volcano Mauna Kea is one of their most sacred places. In 2019, Kanaka Maoli people protested a construction project. A large telescope was going to be built on the volcano.

Many First Nations peoples have also been working to protect their land. For example, Mirarr people are traditional owners of land in northern Australia. For decades, a company has operated a large mine in the area. Mirarr people did not want the mine there. But the mine was set to close in 2021. Mirarr people wanted to decide what to do with the land. In 2018, they won that right.

The cultures of colonizers continue throughout Oceania. For instance, English is an official language in most countries. Christianity is common, too. And most people in Oceania live in

▲ Protesters block a road in protest of a proposed telescope on the volcano Mauna Kea.

cities. These cities are similar to North America's and Europe's cities. In cities, people also tend to be less connected to the land. This difference has been hard for many Indigenous people.

Many immigrant groups also shape Oceania. Since the 2000s, millions of people have moved to the region. These people came from a variety of countries, including China and Vietnam. They bring their own cultures and histories. They make sure that Oceania will always be a changing place.

FOCUS ON
OCEANIA

Write your answers on a separate piece of paper.

1. Write a paragraph describing the main ideas of Chapter 6.

2. The geography of Oceania has affected its history and people in many ways. How has the geography of your area affected the history and people there?

3. Approximately what total area does Oceania cover?

   A. 400,000 square miles (1 million sq km)
   B. 4 million square miles (10 million sq km)
   C. 40 million square miles (100 million sq km)

4. Why might climate change make migration and other kinds of movement in Oceania more common?

   A. Climate change will make some areas less livable.
   B. Climate change will make it cheaper for people to travel.
   C. Climate change will bring wealth to more people.

Answer key on page 48.

GLOSSARY

assimilate
To become part of a group, culture, or society.

atoll
An island created by a coral reef.

biodiversity
The number of different species that live in an area.

climate change
A human-caused global crisis involving long-term changes in Earth's temperature and weather patterns.

colony
An area controlled by a country that is far away.

Indigenous
Native to a region, or belonging to ancestors who lived in a region before colonists arrived.

migration
When humans move from one region to another.

parliamentary democracies
Governments in which a group of elected representatives make laws and in which the prime minister comes out of that group, rather than being elected separately by citizens.

pidgin
A language that combines parts of two or more languages and is used by people who do not speak the same language.

refugees
People forced to leave their homes due to war or other dangers.

TO LEARN MORE

BOOKS

Hamilton, John. *Hawaii*. Minneapolis: Abdo Publishing, 2017.

NgCheong-Lum, Roseline, and Debbie Nevins. *Fiji*. New York: Cavendish Square, 2020.

Walsh Shepherd, Donna. *New Zealand*. New York: Scholastic, 2016.

NOTE TO EDUCATORS

Visit **www.focusreaders.com** to find lesson plans, activities, links, and other resources related to this title.

INDEX

Answer Key: 1. Answers will vary; **2.** Answers will vary; **3.** C; **4.** A